UP A TREE

Three-Toed Sloths

Willow Clark

Published in 2012 by The Rosen Publishing Group, Inc.
29 East 21st Street, New York, NY 10010

First Edition

Editor: Joanne Randolph
Book Design: Greg Tucker
Layout Design: Kate Laczynski

Photo Credits: Cover, pp. 18, 19 Shutterstock.com; pp. 4–5 © www.iStockphoto.com/Erik Gauger; pp. 6, 9 (right), 10, 12–13, 16–17 © Minden Pictures/SuperStock; pp. 8, 14 Roy Toft/Getty Images; p. 9 (left) Norbert Wu/Getty Images; p. 11 Gordon Wiltsie/Getty Images; p. 15 © www.iStockphoto.com/Sergey Dubrovskiy; p. 20 Anna Henly/Getty Images; p. 21 © www.iStockphoto.com/Mark Kostich; p. 22 © www.iStockphoto.com/Pierre Chouinard.

Library of Congress Cataloging-in-Publication Data

Clark, Willow.
 Three-toed sloths / by Willow Clark. — 1st ed.
     p. cm. — (Up a tree)
 Includes index.
 ISBN 978-1-4488-6186-6 (library binding) — ISBN 978-1-4488-6331-0 (pbk.) — ISBN 978-1-4488-6332-7 (6-pack)
 1. Bradypus—Juvenile literature. I. Title.
 QL737.E22C53 2012
 599.3'13—dc23
                        2011028111

Manufactured in the United States of America

CPSIA Compliance Information: Batch #WW12PK: For Further Information contact Rosen Publishing, New York, New York at 1-800-237-9932

Contents

What's in a Name?

The word "sloth" means "laziness." The animals known as sloths are not lazy. These **mammals** are among the slowest-moving animals on Earth, though. There are six **species** of sloths in the world. Two of those species are two-toed sloths, and four of those species are three-toed sloths.

Three-toed sloths live in tropical rain forests in Central America and South America. They are **arboreal** animals, which means they spend most of their lives in trees. This book will teach you more about these slow but fascinating animals.

Sloths have long legs. Their front legs are stronger and longer than their back legs.

Living the High Life

Three-toed sloths live in rain forests from the Central American country of Honduras to Brazil, in South America. Some parts of this habitat are low and near the coasts. Other parts of the rain forests are hillier. The climate in this habitat is warm and wet year-round.

Three-toed sloths are suited to their habitat. They use their long claws to hang upside down from tree branches.

Sloths spend so much time hanging upside down that their fur grows in the opposite direction from most other animals'. This helps direct rain off their bodies.

Where Three-Toed Sloths Live

Atlantic Ocean

SOUTH AMERICA

Pacific Ocean

Atlantic Ocean

MAP KEY

Three-Toed Sloth Range

Sloths mostly stay in the canopy, or in the upper branches of trees in their habitat. Almost everything they need is up in the canopy, including food and places to hang out and sleep!

A Sloth's Body

There are four species of three-toed sloths. They are the brown-throated, the pale-throated, the maned, and the pygmy. These sloths have many things in common. They have small, flat heads, big eyes, stubby tails, and small ears. They have four limbs. All four feet have three long, hook-like claws connected to three **fused digits**.

This is a brown-throated sloth. Brown-throated sloths are the most common kind.

A full-grown sloth is about 20 inches (51 cm) long and weighs between 9 and 11 pounds (4–5 kg). That is about the size of a cat.

Sloths have thick, brownish fur. The fur sometimes has green algae growing on it. That may sound gross, but it gives the sloth **camouflage**!

Quite a Head Turner!

If you hung from a branch, as a sloth does, you would not be able to see much. The human neck can rotate, or turn, only about 80 degrees in either direction. This is enough to let you look over your shoulders.

This sloth is able to look directly behind itself because of the extra bones in its neck.

Sloths, however, have extra **vertebrae**, or bones, in their necks. These extra bones allow sloths to turn their heads 270 degrees in either direction.

Being able to turn its head so far also helps the sloth look for young leaves without using too much energy.

That is three-quarters of a circle! This means sloths can easily see what is going on behind them without having to move the rest of their bodies.

The Facts About Sloths

1

A sloth's grip is so strong that sometimes a sloth stays hanging from a branch even after it has died.

6

Male sloths spend most of their time alone. Female sloths sometimes gather in small groups.

2

Sloths rarely come down to the ground. One reason they do this is to go to the bathroom. They do this only about once each week!

3

Sloths have a lower body temperature than other mammals do. They sometimes sit in the sun to warm up.

4

The pygmy sloth is the smallest three-toed sloth species. It is about 85 percent of the size of other three-toed sloths.

5

Sloths get almost all the water they need from the plants that they eat.

7

Three-toed sloths are also called ai (pronounced "EYE"). They get this nickname for the noise they make when they feel threatened.

8

Two of the sloth's closest animal relatives are armadillos and anteaters.

9

Today's sloths are small, but one of their ancient relatives was a giant ground sloth known as the *Megatherium*. It was as big as an elephant!

Time to Eat!

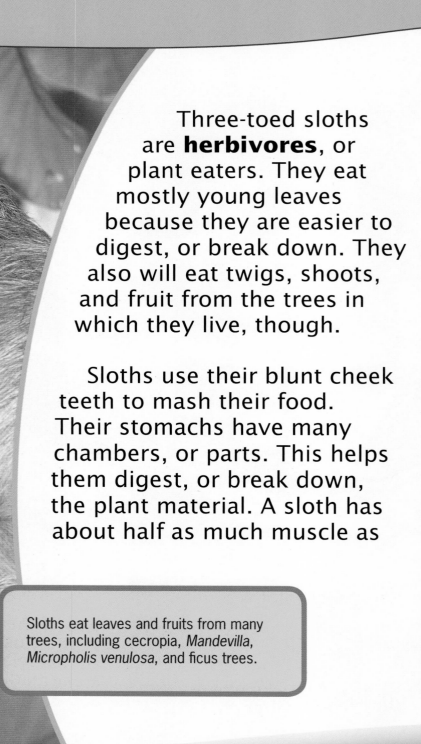

Three-toed sloths are **herbivores**, or plant eaters. They eat mostly young leaves because they are easier to digest, or break down. They also will eat twigs, shoots, and fruit from the trees in which they live, though.

Sloths use their blunt cheek teeth to mash their food. Their stomachs have many chambers, or parts. This helps them digest, or break down, the plant material. A sloth has about half as much muscle as

Sloths eat leaves and fruits from many trees, including cecropia, *Mandevilla*, *Micropholis venulosa*, and ficus trees.

Liana vines climb up rain forest trees and spread to other trees, too. Sloths eat the liana vine leaves, but they also use the vines to climb between trees in the canopy.

other mammals of its size. Having less muscle mass means sloths do not need as much food energy. Luckily, sloths do not need a lot of muscle for their slow-moving lifestyle, so the sloth's diet is suited to its needs.

Life in the Slow Lane

The three-toed sloth's diet does not give it a lot of energy or nutrients. This helps explain why these animals move so slowly and stay still much of the time. Being still also makes it hard for **predators** to see them. On the ground, the sloth's claws and weak back legs make it slow and clumsy. This makes a sloth an easy target for predators.

Sloths may be slow in the trees and on the ground, but they are good swimmers. They use their long arms to paddle through the water.

The sloth's low-energy diet also explains why these **nocturnal** animals sleep between 15 and 20 hours every day. They sleep hanging from branches, using their long claws to hold on.

Sloth Predators

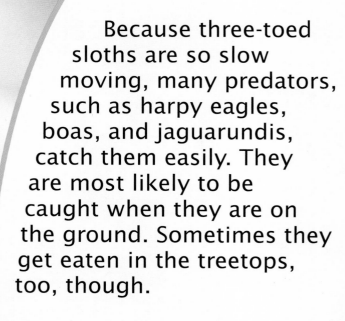

Because three-toed sloths are so slow moving, many predators, such as harpy eagles, boas, and jaguarundis, catch them easily. They are most likely to be caught when they are on the ground. Sometimes they get eaten in the treetops, too, though.

Unlike other animals, sloths cannot run away to escape predators. The only ways a sloth can **protect** itself are by clawing or

Jaguars and their relatives live in many of the same places sloths do and are happy to eat sloths. Jaguars hunt for prey in the trees, on the ground, or in the water.

Harpy eagles are one of the main predators of animals in the rain forest canopy. They are able to move through the trees quickly even with their 6.5-foot (2 m) wingspan.

biting a predator. Its best **defense** is to stay high in the treetops. By moving slowly or staying still, it often goes unnoticed by its predators.

Sloth Babies

Three-toed sloths **mate** between September and November each year. The mother has the baby about six months after mating. She does this while hanging from a branch!

Three-toed sloth babies hang on to their mothers' stomachs until they are old enough to be on their own.

Baby sloths hold tightly to their mothers. They ride along with her as she moves through the trees. For the first four months, the baby drinks its mother's milk. After that, the mother begins to feed her young leaves so that it

Once baby sloths are doing things on their own, they need to be careful to not do things that are too risky. The three-toed sloth's life span in the wild is about 20 years.

will learn what plant material is good to eat. At between 8 and 11 months old, the young leaves its mother to live on its own. It will not be full-grown until it is between two and three years old.

Sloths in Trouble

Sloths face habitat loss as forests are cleared to make way for farms or houses. This leaves sloths with fewer trees in which to make their homes. Some three-toed sloths have been hurt so much by habitat loss that they are **endangered**. Pygmy three-toed sloths are critically endangered. This

People travel to tropical rain forests to see the wildlife, including three-toed sloths. People must be careful not to disturb these gentle animals.

means there are almost none left. They have the smallest range and are most affected by habitat loss and illegal hunting.

People are working to make laws to protect rain forest habitats and animals. The Aviarios Sloth **Sanctuary** of Costa Rica is a safe place for sloths to live and teaches people about these interesting animals.

Glossary

arboreal (ahr-BOR-ee-ul) Having to do with trees.

camouflage (KA-muh-flahj) A color or shape that matches what is around something and helps hide it.

defense (dih-FENTS) Something a living thing does that helps keep it safe.

digits (DIH-jits) Fingers and toes.

endangered (in-DAYN-jerd) Describing an animal whose species or group has almost all died out.

fused (FYOOZD) Joined together.

herbivores (ER-buh-vorz) Animals that eat only plants.

mammals (MA-mulz) Warm-blooded animals that have backbones and hair, breathe air, and feed milk to their young.

mate (MAYT) To come together to make babies.

nocturnal (nok-TUR-nul) Active during the night.

predators (PREH-duh-terz) Animals that kill other animals for food.

protect (pruh-TEKT) To keep safe.

sanctuary (SANK-choo-weh-ree) A safe place.

species (SPEE-sheez) One kind of living thing. All people are one species.

vertebrae (VER-tuh-bray) Backbones, which protect the spinal cord.

Index

Web Sites

Due to the changing nature of Internet links, PowerKids Press has developed an online list of Web sites related to the subject of this book. This site is updated regularly. Please use this link to access the list:
www.powerkidslinks.com/uptr/sloth/